Wildflowers
of the Shenandoah Valley
and Blue Ridge Mountains

Wildflowers
of the Shenandoah Valley
and Blue Ridge Mountains

Oscar W. Gupton and Fred C. Swope
Department of Biology
Virginia Military Institute

University Press of Virginia
Charlottesville

THE UNIVERSITY PRESS OF VIRGINIA
Copyright © 1979 by the Rector and Visitors
of the University of Virginia

Fourth printing 1993

Library of Congress Cataloging in Publication Data
Gupton, Oscar W.
   Wildflowers of the Shenandoah Valley and Blue Ridge Mountains.
   Includes indexes.
     1. Wild flowers—Virginia—Identification.
   2. Wild flowers—Shenandoah Valley—Identification.
   3. Wild flowers—Blue Ridge Mountains—Identification.   I. Swope,
Fred C., joint author.   II. Title.
QK191.G89   582'.13'09755   78–21296
ISBN 0–8139–0814–0

Printed in Hong Kong

To

Caroline	Diane
Caroline T.	Laura A.
Craig	Martin

Contents

Introduction

The first American-born naturalist of note, John Bartram, collected many plants from much of the eastern United States for shipment to Europe, but there was one special place that yielded a wealth of wildflower specimens evidencing the beauty and diversity of plant life in the New World. Our colonial botanist wrote often of the excellence of this choice region; yet he was reluctant to reveal its location to anyone. Bartram's floral gold mine we now know as the Shenandoah Valley. This valley and the adjacent Blue Ridge Mountains have remained as favorite haunts of wildflower enthusiasts from the early days of this country to the present day and are cited frequently for their richness as natural gardens of Virginia.

The plants included here are part of the flora of this mountain-valley region. Some are native to the area, and some are introductions that have become established here. Many of these can be seen along the roadsides, in open fields, and at the borders of wooded areas, while others require a hike off the road to habitats that have been left relatively undisturbed. Most are fairly common or not too infrequently encountered, but there are a few species that are just not plentiful anywhere.

Ever-increasing awareness of ecological problems has brought concern for the status of our environment, for our concept of progress, and for our blindness to the interdependencies of the forces of nature. Any attempt to gain an appreciation of these things requires an understanding of the other forms of life that share our world, and this must begin with identification of some of the kinds of organisms around us.

This book is designed as an aid in the identification of some of the wildflowers by those without previous training in plant biology. Color photographs taken in the field under natural light conditions are arranged according to flower color along with an indication of the size of the photograph relative to the actual size of the plant. The descriptions of each plant are written in nontechnical language requiring neither background information about plant structure nor the use of a glossary or diagram.

This volume comprises photographs of two hundred species of mainly herbaceous plants with a very few woody vines and small shrubs. The rhododendrons and mountain laurel are sizable shrubs but are depicted here because they are so frequently included in any description of this area. The plants pictured here then are those usually called "wildflowers." There are 176 genera and 60 families represented by the photographed species, and there are 85 citations of additional species with respect to their distinguishing features. Thus there is a guide to the identification of 285 species of plants of the region indicated on the following map. These plants, for the most part, are found in the territories ranging in all directions from here; consequently the usefulness of the guide is by no means limited to the immediate area.

OSCAR W. GUPTON
FRED C. SWOPE

Lexington, Virginia

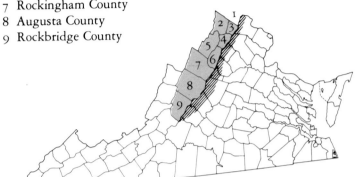

1 Blue Ridge Mountains
2 Frederick County
3 Clarke County
4 Warren County
5 Shenandoah County
6 Page County
7 Rockingham County
8 Augusta County
9 Rockbridge County

Format

The plants are arranged in nine groups according to flower color in the following order: white, green, yellow, orange, pink, red, blue, purple, and either pink or red with yellow. The size of the photograph relative to the actual size of the plant is indicated by a magnification symbol. The symbol $\times 2$, for example, means that the size of the photograph is twice that of the plant; $\times 1$ means that the photograph is the same size as the plant; and $\times \frac{1}{2}$ means that the photograph is one half the size of the plant.

Within each of the flower color groups the plants are arranged in order of the time of flowering.

The information pertaining to each species is given in the same order throughout:

Common name of species

Scientific name of species	Common name of family	Scientific name of family
Flowering period	Frequency (common, infrequent, rare)	

Description:

Size is indicated by a statement of the overall height of the plant or, in the case of vines, whether they are low- or high-climbing.

Leaf character is given in terms of size, shape, number, arrangement, or other feature peculiar to the plant.

Flower color variations are noted.

Other species similar to the one depicted are cited along with their distinguishing features.

Medicinal or food value or reputed value is noted.

Poisonous nature is indicated if sickness or death has resulted from eating or if skin inflammation has resulted from handling. This entry is made if the species is toxic to humans or other animals.

Miscellaneous general interest notes may be included.

Habitat or type of environment in which the plant is usually found is characterized.

The scientific names follow the eighth edition of *Gray's Manual of Botany*, and a guide to pronunciation is furnished.

The works listed below are plant manuals with keys consisting of technical information for identification of the plants of the northeastern United States.

Fernald, M. L. 1950. *Gray's Manual of Botany*. Eighth edition. American Book Company.

Gleason, M. A. 1952. *Illustrated Flora of the Northeastern United States and Adjacent Canada*. The New York Botanical Garden.

Gleason, M. A., and A. Cronquist. 1963. *Manual of the Vascular Plants of Northeastern United States and Adjacent Canada*. D. Van Nostrand Company.

Rickett, N. W. 1953. *Wildflowers of the United States*. Crown Publishers.

Wildflowers
of the Shenandoah Valley
and Blue Ridge Mountains

×⅔

Bloodroot

Sanguinaria canadensis

Poppy Family *Papaveraceae*

March–April

Common

From 2 to 8 inches tall. Usually 1 round and variously lobed leaf is folded around the flowering stalk. The underground stem contains the "blood" referred to in the name. The plant is poisonous if eaten and a skin irritant to some.

Rich woods, steep slopes.

×½

Toothwort

Dentaria laciniata   Mustard Family   *Cruciferae*

March—May   Common

From 6 to 12 inches tall, with 3 leaves in a whorl below the flower, no basal leaves. Flowers may be white or pink. *D. diphylla* and *D. heterophylla* are similar but have basal leaves; the former has much more rounded leaves, while the latter is similar to the pictured leaves.

Rich, wooded slopes and bottoms.

×½

Liverwort

Hepatica acutiloba   Crowfoot Family   *Ranunculaceae*

March–May   Common

From 1 to 6 inches tall. New leaves appear after the flowers. Flowers vary from white to pink or blue. Another species, *H. americana*, is very similar but has rounded leaf lobes. Leaves were thought to have medicinal value for liver ailments.

Rich woods.

×½

Twinleaf

Jeffersonia diphylla Barberry Family *Berberidaceae*

April–May Rare

From 8 to 12 inches tall. Leaves are deeply divided and resemble butterflies. This plant was named for Thomas Jeffer-
son, the third president of the United States and the founder
of the University of Virginia.

Rich, wooded slopes with limestone soil.

×⅔

Dutchman's Breeches

Dicentra cucullaria

April–May

Poppy Family   *Papaveraceae*

Infrequent

From 6 to 12 inches tall. Leaves are much dissected and fernlike with a light or whitish green color and pink or red stalks. Another species, *D. canadensis*, has the same leaf appearance and flower color, but the "breeches" have shorter "legs." The flower clusters resemble clothes hanging out to dry. All species of this genus are poisonous to cattle.

Rich woods.

×1⅓

Rue Anemone

Anemonella thalictroides   Crowfoot Family   *Ranunculaceae*

April—May   Common

From 3 to 8 inches tall, with leaves only at base of stem and immediately beneath flowers. Leaves are divided into small segments with usually 3 lobes. Flower color may vary from white to pinkish blue.

Open woods.

×⅔

Sweet Cicely

Osmorhiza claytoni

April–May

Parsley Family *Umbelliferae*

Common

From 1 to 3 feet tall. Leaves are divided into groups of 3 pointed and toothed segments. The roots and stems have the odor and taste of licorice. However, another plant is the source of true licorice.

Stream banks, moist woods.

×¾

Pussy-toes

Antennaria plantaginifolia   Composite Family   *Compositae*

April–June   Common

From 4 to 14 inches tall. Leaves are mostly basal with the upper stem leaves much smaller. These plants have separate sex; female flowering heads are a little longer and more cylindrical than the pictured male. There is another species, *A. solitaria*, with only a single flowering head.

Dry, open woods and fields.

×⅔

Garlic Mustard

Alliaria officinalis   Mustard Family   *Cruciferae*

April–June   Infrequent

From 2 to 3 foot straight and slender stem, with triangular or oval leaves and the odor of onion or garlic. This European introduction has been used in salads and as a medicine. It gives its flavor to cow's milk.

Moist, open woods and roadsides.

×½

Wild Strawberry

Fragaria virginiana   Rose Family   *Rosaceae*

April—June   Common

From 3 to 10 inches tall. Leaves are divided into 3 toothed segments. Fruits are a smaller edition of the garden straw-berry, × *F. ananassa*, which is a hybrid of this species and *F. chiloensis*. Wild strawberries usually have a sharper flavor than the garden strawberry. The Indian strawberry, *Duches-nea indica*, is similar but with yellow flowers and tasteless fruits.

Fields, wood borders, roadsides.

×1

Star-of-Bethlehem

Ornithogalum umbellatum   Lily Family *Liliaceae*

April—June   Infrequent

From 4 to 10 inches tall. Leaves are grasslike. This is a European introduction escaped from cultivation in gardens. It is attractive but is poisonous if taken internally.

Roadsides, fields, and wood borders.

×½

May-apple

Podophyllum peltatum Barberry Family *Berberidaceae*

April–June Common

From 8 inches to about 1½ feet tall. Leaves are large and umbrellalike. Flowering stems have 2 leaves with the flower between. The ripe fruits are edible, but unripe fruits and the rest of the plant are poisonous if eaten. Underground parts also cause skin irritation.

Moist woods, roadsides.

12

×¾

Bishop's Cap

Mitella diphylla

April–June

Saxifrage Family *Saxifragaceae*

Common

From 8 inches to 2 feet tall, with straight slender stem and basal leaves ovate or heart-shaped with long stalks. On the stem below the flowers are two smaller leaves with either no stalks or short ones. The name refers to the shape of the fruit.

Rich woods, stream banks.

13

×1½

Great Chickweed

Stellaria pubera

Pink Family *Caryophyllaceae*

April–June Common

Early plants from 4 to 10 inches tall, later growing to a height of 2 feet. Leaves are in pairs and ovate, often the widest part nearest the tip. They are generally found in rather dense tufts.

Woods, wooded roadside banks.

×1

Wood Vetch

Vicia caroliniana   Bean Family   *Leguminosae*

April–June   Infrequent

From 1 to 3 feet tall, trailing along the ground or climbing. Leaves are divided into narrow segments with threadlike curling tendrils at the tip. Flower color varies from white to pale blue. This is one of our few native vetches.

Woods, wood borders, roadsides.

15

×½

Large-flowered Trillium

Trillium grandiflorum   Lily Family *Liliaceae*

April–June   Common

From 8 inches to 1½ feet tall. Flower color is highly variable
from white to deep red-pink. There are several trilliums easily recognized by the parts in threes; this species is usually
considered the most showy. *T. undulatum* has white flowers
with purple streaks.

Rich woods, often in coves, on slopes.

×1

Watercress

Nasturtium officinale   Mustard Family   *Cruciferae*

April–July   Common

From 6 inches to 2½ feet tall, with stems and leaves lying on the ground or floating on water and many roots growing from stem at leaf bases. Leaves are divided into several nearly round segments. It is used as salad green. This plant is no relation to the garden nasturtium, *Tropaeolum majus*, which is not a part of our flora.

In streams or springs or the wet soil immediately around them.

× 1½

Wild Lily of the Valley

Maianthemum canadense   Lily Family   *Liliaceae*

May–June   Common

From 2 to 8 inches tall, usually with 2 ovate leaves without stalks or with very short stalks, clasping the stem. Many times these plants are found in extensive carpetlike colonies.

Moist woods.

18

×⅔

Solomon's Seal

Polygonatum biflorum   Lily Family   *Liliaceae*

May–June   Common

From 1 to 4 feet tall. Leaves are without stalks in 2 rows along the stem and pointed. Flower color is white to greenish or yellowish white. *P. pubescens* is similar but with hairy leaves.

Moist woods.

×¾

False Solomon's Seal

Smilacina racemosa   Lily Family   *Liliaceae*

May–June   Common

From 1 to 3 feet tall. Leaves are in 2 rows along the stem with very short stalks. It is similar to Solomon's seal, *Polygonatum biflorum*, except that the flowers are at the end of the stem rather than along the lower side of the stem.

Moist woods, roadside banks.

×1½

Stonecrop

Sedum ternatum   Orpine Family   *Crassulaceae*

May–June   Infrequent

From 2 to 8 inches tall. Leaves are spoon-shaped to round, many in whorls of 3. These plants are usually found in dense mats often covering large areas.

Rock outcrops, rocky slopes, woods.

×¾

Lily of the Valley

Convallaria majalis   Lily Family   *Liliaceae*

May–June   Rare

From 4 to 10 inches tall. Leaves are large and sheath the stem. These plants are usually found in dense colonies. The plants are poisonous if eaten and are skin irritants to some.

Roadsides, open woods.

×1

Bastard Toadflax

Comandra umbellata   Sandalwood Family   *Santalaceae*

May–June   Infrequent

From 6 to 16 inches tall. Leaves are narrowly oval, tapering at both ends. Small to extensive colonies are found. These plants are parasitic upon the roots of woody plants.

Dry open woods.

23

×½

Speckled Wood Lily

Clintonia umbellulata Lily Family *Liliaceae*

May–June Common

From 8 inches to 1½ feet tall, with all basal leaves and a group of 5 to 30 flowers with the stalks all arising from the same place. The petals are spotted. *C. borealis* is similar but with yellow flowers.

Rich woods.

×½

Carrion Flower

Smilax herbacea   Lily Family   *Liliaceae*

May–June   Common

A climbing vine to 7 feet in length, often forming a tangle
of stems. Leaves are rounded-triangular or heart-shaped to
almost round, and flowers have an unpleasant odor. There
are other similar members of this group (catbriers or green-
briers) but with woody stems and prickles.

Moist woods, low roadsides.

×1¼

Foamflower

Tiarella cordifolia   Saxifrage Family   *Saxifragaceae*

May–June   Infrequent

From 4 inches to 1 foot tall. Leaves are all basal and heart-shaped to almost round, their margins unevenly lobed and toothed.

Rich woods, steep wooded slopes, roadside banks.

×¾

Deerberry

Vaccinium stamineum   Heath Family   *Ericaceae*

May–June   Common

From 1 to 6 feet tall. Leaves are oblong or ovate, often with the widest part nearest the tip and whitish beneath. The long stamens give the flowers a tassel effect. The fruits are larger than blueberries, which are in this group; they are bitter but are said to make fine jam.

Dry woods.

×1

Low Bindweed

Convolvulus spithamaeus   Morning Glory Family   *Convolvulaceae*

May–July   Common

From 3 inches to 1½ feet tall, sometimes bending back to the ground. Leaves are oval to arrowhead-shaped and usually hairy. Flowers are commonly white but occasionally have a pink tinge.

Roadsides, fields.

×1⅓

Bowman's Root

Gillenia trifoliata   Rose Family   *Rosaceae*

May–July   Common

From 1½ to 3½ feet tall. Leaves are divided into 3 toothed and pointed segments. It contains an emetic and has been used medicinally.

Woods, roadside banks.

29

×1¼

Canada Violet

Viola canadensis   Violet Family   *Violaceae*

May–July   Common

From 8 inches to over 1 foot tall, with several stems with many leaves and several long-stalked basal leaves. Flowers vary from white inside and purple-tinted outside to all pale purple.

Rich woods, rocky wooded slopes.

×⅔

Galax

Galax aphylla   Diapensia Family   *Diapensiaceae*

June–July   Infrequent

From 10 inches to 2 feet tall. Heart-shaped to almost round leaves are all basal and toothed. There is usually a cluster of leaves from which the leafless flower stalk arises.

Open woods, rocky slopes.

31

× ¹/₅

Cow Parsnip

Heracleum maximum   Parsley Family   *Umbelliferae*

June–July   Infrequent

From 3 to 10 feet tall, with very large stems, leaves, and flower heads. Leaves are divided into three segments, and base of leaf stalk is much widened. Flower heads are 4 to 10 inches in diameter. Reportedly poisonous if taken internally. Skin irritant.

Streamsides, moist roadsides.

×¼

Fly Poison

Amianthium muscaetoxicum   Lily Family *Liliaceae*

June–July   Common

From 1 to 3 feet tall. Straplike basal leaves are 1 foot or more in length. Flower color varies from white to green as the fruits begin to form. The plant is poisonous if taken internally.

Wet to somewhat dry open woods.

×½

Goat's Beard

Aruncus dioicus   Rose Family   *Rosaceae*

June–July   Common

From 3 to 6 feet tall. Leaves are very large and divided into many segments. This plant is very similar to false goat's beard, *Astilbe biternata*, which has the leaf segment at tip of leaf usually in three or more lobes.

Roadsides, wood borders.

34

×½

New Jersey Tea

Ceanothus americanus   Buckthorn Family   *Rhamnaceae*

June–July   Common

From 2 to 3 feet tall. Leaves oval, tapering at both ends, and veins underneath the leaf base seem to run off the blade of the leaf. Leaves were used for making tea during the American Revolution.

Open woods, roadsides.

×⅔

Tassel Rue

Trautvetteria caroliniensis   Crowfoot Family   *Ranunculaceae*

June–July   Infrequent

From 1½ to 5 feet tall. Leaves are large, almost round with many lobes and teeth, upper leaves without stalks, lower leaves with long stalks. The many stamens give a tassel effect to the flowers.

Low moist woods, stream banks.

×½

Ginseng

Panax quinquefolius   Ginseng Family   *Araliaceae*

June–July   Rare

From 8 inches to 2 feet tall, with a whorl of 3 or 4 usually 5-parted toothed leaves. The fruit is bright red. *P. trifolius* is smaller with usually 3 stalkless leaves. The species pictured here is valued highly by the Chinese as a medicine.

Rich woods.

×1⅓

Spotted Wintergreen

Chimaphila maculata　　　　Wintergreen Family　*Pyrolaceae*

June–August　　　　　　　Common

From 3 to 10 inches tall. Leaves are dark green with whitish markings, toothed and tapering to a point. Flowers are fragrant. Prince's pine, *C. umbellata*, is similar with leaves a little larger and without the white markings.

Dry woods.

× ¹/₆

Bear Grass

Yucca filamentosa

Lily Family   *Liliaceae*

June–August

Infrequent

From 3 to 8 feet tall. Leaves are long, narrow, and sharp-pointed, clustered at base and reduced up the stem. This is a coastal plain species that has been cultivated and escaped.

Roadsides, open woods, fields.

39

×⅔

Hedge Bindweed

Convolvulus sepium   Morning Glory Family   *Convolvulaceae*

June–August   Infrequent

A trailing or twining vine, with leaves triangular to oval. Flowers vary from white to pink or pinkish blue. It has been reported to be at least slightly poisonous, perhaps only to swine.

Roadsides, fields.

×1

Ox-eye Daisy

Chrysanthemum leucanthemum   Composite Family   *Compositae*

June–August   Common

From 8 inches to 2½ feet tall, with several basal leaves that
are larger at the tip, stem leaves smaller, and all leaves irregularly toothed or lobed. Many times it occurs in large
colonies.

Roadsides, fields.

×¹⁄₆

Black Snakeroot

Cimicifuga racemosa   Crowfoot Family   *Ranunculaceae*

June–August   Common

From 3 to 8 feet tall. Large leaves are divided into several units of 3 lobed and toothed segments. Flowering stalks may reach 3 feet in length. Another species, *C. americana*, is very similar except for floral details and a little later flowering period.

Rich woods.

×¾

Button Bush

Cephalanthus occidentalis   Madder Family   *Rubiaceae*

June–August   Infrequent

From 3 to 10 feet tall. Oblong and pointed leaves are usually in pairs but sometimes in groups of three or four. The plant is poisonous if eaten.

Streamsides, ponds, swamps.

43

×⅔

Wild Quinine

Parthenium integrifolium Composite Family *Compositae*

June–August Common

From 1 to 4 feet tall. Basal leaves are large and ovate with rounded teeth; upper leaves are much smaller and without stalks. A Mexican species has been used as a source of rubber.

Roadsides, open woods, fields.

×¾

Yarrow

Achillea millefolium Composite Family *Compositae*

June–September Common

From 8 inches to 3 feet tall. Leaves are finely divided into very small segments, giving a fernlike appearance. Flower color may vary from white to pink. It has an odor described by some as aromatic and has been used medicinally.

Roadsides, fields, wood borders.

45

×1⅓

Water Willow

Justicia americana   Acanthus Family   *Acanthaceae*

June—September   Infrequent

From 1 to 3 feet tall, with narrow leaves in pairs and 2 or
more flowers supported by a 2- to 6-inch stalk from upper
leaf axils. Flower color varies from purple to white with deep
purple markings.

Shallow streams, wet stream margins.

×½

Queen Anne's Lace

Daucus carota   Parsley Family   *Umbelliferae*

June–September   Common

From 1 to 5 feet tall. Leaves are large but divided into many small narrow segments. The central flower of each flowering head is often red or purple. The cultivated carrot is a form of this species. It lends a sour taste to cow's milk and is sometimes a skin irritant.

Roadsides, fields.

×¾

Flowering Spurge

Euphorbia corollata

June–October

Spurge Family *Euphorbiaceae*

Common

From 1 to 3 feet tall and usually with several branches. Leaves are oval, varying from narrow to almost round. The "flowers" are clusters of tiny flowers with surrounding pet-allike appendages. The sap is milky and poisonous internally and externally. The Christmas flower, poinsettia, is a member of this plant group.

Roadsides, fields, open woods.

×1

Indian Pipe

Monotropa uniflora   Heath Family   *Pyrolaceae*

June–October   Infrequent

From 3 inches to 1 foot tall, with scalelike leaves and one flower per stem. The plant is white, pink, yellow, or blue in varying shades and combinations. No chlorophyll is produced; food is obtained from other plants. It contains a poisonous substance common to many members of the family.

Wooded slopes.

×2

Wintergreen

Gaultheria procumbens   Heath Family   *Ericaceae*

July–August   Common

From 3 to 8 inches tall. Leaves are glossy and oval, crowded toward the tip of the stem. The fruit is a bright red berry. This plant is a source of oil of wintergreen and has this odor when crushed. The leaves have been used for making a tea.

Dry or moist wooded areas.

× 1¼

Buttonweed

Malva rotundifolia Mallow Family *Malvaceae*

July–August Common

From 6 inches to 3 feet tall. Stems usually trail along the ground, and leaves are long-stalked and round to heart-shaped with slightly lobed margins. The flower color varies from white to pale pink or blue.

Roadsides, fields.

×¾

Starry Campion

Silene stellata   Pink Family   *Caryophyllaceae*

July–September   Infrequent

From 1 to 4 feet tall, with leaves midway up the stem in whorls of 4 and other leaves in pairs. *S. cucubalus* flowers a little earlier and is similar but with opposite leaves only, petals only 2-lobed, and flower base appearing inflated.

Rich woods.

× 1½

Doll's Eyes

Actaea pachypoda   Crowfoot Family   *Ranunculaceae*

July–September (fruiting)   Infrequent

From 1 to 3 feet tall. Large leaves are divided into groups of 3 toothed and pointed segments. Flowering occurs in May and June with a leafless, long flowering stalk arising from the stem tip and ending in an oval cluster of small white flowers. *A. rubra* has red fruits, and both species may be red or white; however, the thicker fruit stalks of the pictured plant are distinctive. Both species are very poisonous.

Rich woods, wooded roadside banks.

×⅔

Jimson Weed

Datura stramonium　　　　　Nightshade Family　*Solanaceae*

July–October　　　　　Common

From 1½ to 5 feet tall. Stem is often purple, and leaves are ovate with large teeth. Flower color varies from white to bluish. Fruits are spiny. The plant is poisonous both externally and internally.

Roadsides, fields, pastures.

×1

Slender Ladies' Tresses

Spiranthes gracilis   Orchid Family   *Orchidaceae*

August–September   Infrequent

From 4 inches to 2½ feet tall. Leaves are small and scalelike, and oval basal leaves are usually absent at flowering. Lower part of flowers green and white. *S. tuberosa* is similar but with no green on lower flower parts.

Open woods, fields.

×⅔

Blue Cohosh

Caulophyllum thalictroides   Barberry Family   *Berberidaceae*

May–June   Common

From 1 to 3 feet tall. The plant is blue-green, with 2 very large leaves divided into several groups of 3 segments. Flower color varies from greenish yellow to greenish brown. The fruits appear to be 2 dark blue berries but are actually the seeds that have grown through the fruit wall. It is poisonous.

Rich woods.

×¾

Jack-in-the-pulpit

Arisaema triphyllum　　　　　　Arum Family　*Araceae*

May–July　　　　　　　　　　Common

From 1 to 3 feet tall, with usually 2 leaves divided into 3 or 5 segments. *A. dracontium* has 5- to 15-parted leaves, and "Jack" is taller than the "pulpit." These plants are poisonous if eaten and may result in skin irritation upon handling. Underground parts, however, are edible after cooking.

Moist woods, bogs.

×½

False Hellebore

Veratrum viride   Lily Family   *Liliaceae*

June–July   Infrequent

From 2 to 7 feet tall. Stem is thick; leaves are numerous and pleated with bases clasping the stem. It is poisonous if eaten and may act as a skin irritant. *V. parviflorum* is similar but smaller with stalked leaves and is also poisonous.

Wet woods, swamps.

×½

Poison Ivy

Rhus radicans   Cashew Family   *Anacardiaceae*

June–July   Common

Small and shrubby becoming a trailing or climbing vine.
Leaves are divided into 3 segments. It is confused with
young box elder which has leaves opposite on the stem,
while poison ivy has alternate ones. Extremely poisonous
causing severe skin irritation.

Woods, fields, roadsides, almost anywhere.

×½

Bottlebrush Grass

Hystrix patula

June–August

Grass Family   *Gramineae*

Common

From 1 to 5 feet tall. Leaves are to 1 foot long. Stems and leaves are typical of grasses in general structure. The plant often grows in dense stands. It is interesting to compare the appearance of the flowering head of this plant with the animal member of a group also called *Hystrix*—the porcupine.

Rich woods, low roadsides.

× 1¼

Stinging Nettle

Urtica dioica

June–September

Nettle Family   *Urticaceae*

Common

From 1 to 4 feet tall, with stems and leaves with stinging hairs. Leaves are in pairs with long stalks, elongated heart-shaped with toothed margins. The wood nettle, *Laportea canadensis*, is somewhat similar but leaves not in pairs. Itching is short-lived.

Low woods, stream banks, roadsides.

× 1⅓

Cranefly Orchid

Tipularia discolor　　　　　　Orchid Family　*Orchidaceae*

July–August　　　　　　　Infrequent

From 4 inches to 2 feet tall. Leaves are absent at flowering except for 1 or more sheathing scales at base of flowering stalk. Flower color may vary from green or greenish yellow to brown or purplish brown.

Rich woods.

×⅔

Dog-tooth Violet

Erythronium americanum

March–April

Lily Family   *Liliaceae*

Common

From 2 to 6 inches tall, with 2 leaves near the base spotted with brown. Flower color may vary from yellow to yellowish brown, pink, or occasionally white. These plants are usually found in rather large colonies.

Rich woods.

×¾

Coltsfoot

Tussilago farfara

March–June

Composite Family   *Compositae*

Infrequent

From 2 inches to 1½ feet tall. Flowering stem has scalelike leaves. Basal leaves develop later that are long-stalked and heart-shaped to almost round with teeth. A Eurasian introduction that has migrated steadily southward.

Roadside ditches, streamsides.

×⅓

Dandelion

Taraxacum officinale   Composite Family   *Compositae*

March–October   Common

From 2 inches to 2 feet tall. Leaves are basal and have large irregular teeth or lobes. The plant has been used medicinally and for wine and salad greens.

Roadsides, fields, lawns.

×1

Smooth Yellow Violet

Viola pensylvanica　　　　　　　Violet Family　*Violaceae*

April–May　　　　　　　　　　Infrequent

From 6 inches to 1½ feet tall. Basal leaves are kidney-shaped; stem leaves are rounded to heart-shaped. Another yellow violet, *V. hastata*, has 2 to 4 narrow, sharp-pointed leaves near the top of the stem.

Rich woods, wooded rocky slopes.

×½

Bellwort

Uvularia grandiflora   Lily Family   *Liliaceae*

April–May   Common

From 8 inches to 2 feet tall. Stem seems to pass through the leaves, which are finely hairy underneath. *U. perfoliata* and *U. pudica* are common species; the former has no hair on the leaves, and the latter's stem does not pass through the leaf.

Rich woods, especially limestone soils.

×¾

Marsh Marigold

Caltha palustris   Crowfoot Family   *Ranunculaceae*

April–June   Rare

From 6 inches to 2 feet tall, with hollow stems. Basal leaves are long-stalked and almost round to kidney-shaped with a toothed margin; stem leaves are smaller. It has been used as a cooked green but is poisonous when fresh and gives a bad taste to cow's milk.

Marshes.

× 1¼

Green and Gold

Chrysogonum virginianum Composite Family *Compositae*

April–June Infrequent

Flowers at first almost at ground level, later at a height of 1 to 1½ feet. Leaves are ovate to almost round with small teeth and long stalks.

Woodlands and open wood borders, clearings.

69

× 1½

Stargrass

Hypoxis hirsuta   Amaryllis Family   *Amaryllidaceae*

April–June   Common

From 2 to 8 inches tall. Leaves are hairy and grasslike, taller than the flowers. Flowers are in clusters on the plant with the stalks in each cluster arising from about the same point.

Open woods, roadside banks.

×1

Lousewort

Pedicularis canadensis Figwort Family *Scrophulariaceae*

April–June Common

From 4 inches to 1½ feet tall. Leaves are narrow and deeply lobed. Flowers may be yellow, red-purple, or a combination of both colors.

Open woods, roadside banks.

×¾

Bulbous Buttercup

Ranunculus bulbosus Crowfoot Family *Ranunculaceae*

April–June Common

From 4 inches to 2 feet tall. Base of stem is thickened so as to appear bulblike. The several species of buttercups are generally very similar; the fruits are used to separate them. Most buttercups are poisonous if eaten, and some, including this one, cause skin irritation in some people.

Fields, roadsides, lawns.

×½

Golden Ragwort

Senecio aureus   Composite Family   *Compositae*

April–June   Common

From 1 to over 2½ feet tall. Basal leaves are largest and heart-shaped; there are several to many flower heads. This species and other ragworts are poisonous if eaten.

Moist woods and stream banks.

×1¼

Swallowwort

Chelidonium majus   Poppy Family *Papaveraceae*

April–July   Infrequent

From 1 to 3 feet tall, with erect but spreading habit, yellow-ish orange sap, and leaves divided into many toothed segments. The sap was once recommended as eye medicine, since birds were thought to so treat their young, but the plant is poisonous internally and externally.

Shaded, moist wood borders and stream banks.

Yellow Lady's Slipper

Cypripedium calceolus   Orchid Family   *Orchidaceae*

May–June   Infrequent

From 8 inches to 2½ feet tall. Stem is leafy up to just beneath the flower. Flowers vary from deep, golden yellow to
almost white. Stem and leaves contain a poisonous substance
causing skin irritation similar to poison ivy. Queen lady's
slipper, *C. reginae*, is likewise poisonous; this is a very rare
plant with a pink and white "slipper."

Wooded slopes.

×⅔

Golden Alexander

Zizia aptera   Parsley Family   *Umbelliferae*

May–June   Common

From 8 inches to 2½ feet tall. Basal leaves are heart-shaped generally with occasionally a 3-parted one. This species is similar to the meadow parsnips (*Thaspium*) except that the central flower in each of the small groups making up the flowering head has no stalk.

Open woods and clearings.

×¾

Goat's Beard

Tragopogon major

May–July

Composite Family   *Compositae*

Infrequent

From 1 to 3 feet tall. Leaves are long and narrow, clasping the stem. There is another very similar species, *T. porrifolius*, with purple flowers.

Roadsides, fields.

×¾

Cancer Root

Conopholis americana   Broom Rape Family   *Orobanchaceae*

May–August   Common

From 4 to 10 inches tall, resembling a yellow-brown pine-cone, particularly before the flowers are fully open. The first Latin name means "cone scale." The plants are found in dense colonies usually under the oaks they parasitize.

Woods, usually oak.

×½

Sweet Clover

Melilotus officinalis   Bean Family   *Leguminosae*

May–October   Common

From 1½ to 6 feet tall. Leaves are divided into 3 segments with small teeth and are fragrant. *M. alba* is almost identical except for the white flowers. It has been used as a medicine and a flavoring. Poisoning occurs sometimes when it is used as hay.

Roadsides, fields.

× ⅓

Wild Parsnip

Pastinaca sativa   Parsley Family   *Umbelliferae*

June–July   Infrequent

From 3 to 6 feet tall. Leaves are divided into pairs of toothed or lobed segments; also leaf stalks usually sheath the stem. Flowers are in many clusters with the flower stalks of each cluster all arising from the same point. The plant is a cause of skin irritation to some individuals.

Roadsides, fields.

×⅔

Prickly Pear

Opuntia humifusa   Cactus Family   *Cactaceae*

June–July   Infrequent

From 4 inches to 1½ feet tall, usually found in small to extensive colonies. Handling of this plant results in contact with the tufts of very fine, short hairlike spines that very easily penetrate the skin. The red-purple fruits are edible when the skin is removed.

Sandy, rocky open areas.

× 2/3

Downy False Foxglove

Gerardia virginica   Figwort Family   *Scrophulariaceae*

June–July   Common

From 1 to 4 feet tall. Leaves are in pairs tapering to a point and widest near the base, the margins uneven and often lobed. These plants are parasitic upon oak roots. There are other species with yellow or purple flowers similar to the flowers of this species.

Dry woods.

Indian Cucumber-root

Medeola virginiana　　　　　　　　Lily Family　*Liliaceae*

June–July　　　　　　　　　　　　Common

From 8 inches to 3 feet tall, with 5 to 12 leaves in a whorl about midway up the stem and a whorl of 3 leaves under the flowers. The underground stem is edible and was once thought to have medicinal value.

Rich woods, stream banks.

×1¼

Whorled Loosestrife

Lysimachia quadrifolia   Primrose Family   *Primulaceae*

June–July   Common

From 1 to 3 feet tall, with leaves in whorls of 4 around stem (number may vary). Flower stalks are threadlike. The several loosestrifes all have similar yellow flowers with pointed petals; one, *L. nummularia*, sprawls on the ground unlike the others, and the round leaves suggested its common name, moneywort.

Dry or wet very open woods, clearings.

$\times 1\frac{1}{4}$

Tickseed

Coreopsis verticillata   Composite Family   *Compositae*

June–July   Infrequent

From 1 to 3 feet tall. Leaves are very slender, almost string-like. Tickseeds are similar in the 8-rayed, yellow flower heads; rays are sometimes toothed. *C. major* has paired and cleft leaves giving a whorled appearance. *C. tinctoria* has red or brown spots at base of the yellow rays.

Roadsides, fields, open woods.

× 1¾

Wild Indigo

Baptisia tinctoria   Bean Family   *Leguminosae*

June–August   Common

From 1 to 3 feet tall. Leaves are divided into 3 parts wider near tip. These plants have been used in dyeing, but true indigo dye comes from a different plant. This plant and others of this group have been reported as poisonous.

Wood borders, open woods.

× 1¼

Sundrops

Oenothera fruticosa Evening Primrose Family *Onagraceae*

June–August Common

From 1 to 2½ feet tall. Leaves are more or less pointed at both ends, sometimes rounded, sometimes toothed. *O. tetragona* is very similar but with fruits that are larger in the middle, while this species has fruits larger at upper end.

Roadsides, dry open woods, and wood borders.

×½

Rattlesnake Weed

Hieracium venosum Composite Family *Compositae*

June–August Common

From 8 inches to 3 feet tall. Stem leaves are absent or 1 to 2 highly reduced in size; basal leaves are hairy, oval or larger near the tip, and purple-veined. There are several species in this group that resemble one another strongly in general habit and appearance of flower head.

Open woods, fields.

×1

Butter-and-eggs

Linaria vulgaris   Figwort Family   *Scrophulariaceae*

June–August   Infrequent

From 1 to 3 feet tall, with numerous very narrow light green leaves. Flower color varies from deep yellow to very pale yellow almost white. A European introduction escaped from gardens, this plant frequently forms dense colonies.

Roadsides, fields.

×⅔

Five Finger

Potentilla recta

Rose Family *Rosaceae*

June–August

Common

From 8 inches to 2½ feet tall. Leaves are divided into 5 to 7 segments. Although the several species of five fingers vary somewhat, they have a similar appearance. This species has the largest flowers.

Roadsides, fields.

×⅔

Common St. John's Wort

Hypericum perforatum   St. John's Wort Family   *Guttiferae*

June–September   Common

From 1 to 2½ feet tall. Flowers have black dots, and the many stamens give the flower the appearance of having a tassel in the center. The several species are generally similar; this European introduction is the commonest. Some animals are poisoned if they are exposed to bright light after eating this plant.

Roadsides, fields.

×¹⁄₁₀

Common Mullein

Verbascum thapsus   Figwort Family   *Scrophulariaceae*

June–September   Common

From 3 to 6 feet tall. Stem and leaves are thick and hairy
with a blanketlike texture; leaves are about 1 foot long near
the base, decreasing in size up the stem. *V. phlomoides* is
similar but with larger flowers and without leaves continu-
ing onto stem as in this species.

Roadsides, fields.

×1

Pinesap

Monotropa hypopithys   Heath Family   *Pyrolaceae*

June–October   Infrequent

From 3 inches to 1 foot tall. Leaves are scalelike. The plant is rust, yellow, pink, red, or some combination of these colors. More red tends to occur in the later flowering plants. No chlorophyll is produced; food is obtained from other plants. They are usually found in small to fairly large colonies. Poisonous if eaten.

Wooded slopes.

Black-eyed Susan

Rudbeckia hirta   Composite Family *Compositae*

June–October   Common

From 1 to 3 feet tall. Stems and leaves are hairy, and leaves are mostly basal. Stem leaves are narrow and without stalks; basal leaves are larger and long-stalked. *R. laciniata* is found on streamsides and has a lighter center in the flower head and leaves divided into many segments.

Roadsides, fields.

×¾

Moth Mullein

Verbascum blattaria

June–October

Figwort Family   *Scrophulariaceae*

Common

From 1 to 4 feet tall. Leaves are oblong, sometimes pointed and sometimes blunt, with margins wavy or toothed. The flowers may be yellow or white.

Roadsides, fields.

×¾

Wild Senna

Cassia hebecarpa

July–August

Bean Family   *Leguminosae*

Infrequent

From 2 to 6 feet tall. Leaves are divided into 2 rows of paired oblong segments; the lower part of the leaf stalk has a club-shaped gland. *C. marilandica* is similar but with a shorter hemispheric gland. *C. tora* has only 2 or 3 pairs of leaf segments. *C. fasciculata* and *C. nictitans* are smaller plants with smaller leaf segments; the former has flat glands and the latter stalked glands.

Roadsides, streambanks, moist woods.

× 1½

Pale Touch-me-not

Impatiens pallida   Touch-me-not Family   *Balsaminaceae*

July–September   Common

From 2 to 6 feet tall. Leaves are ovate with rounded teeth, pale green, and soft. The spotted touch-me-not, *I. capensis*, is almost identical but has orange flowers. The sap is said to alleviate poison ivy irritation. Ripe fruits "explode" on handling.

Moist woods, streamsides.

×¾

Three-leaved Rosinweed

Silphium trifoliatum   Composite Family   *Compositae*

July–September   Common

From 4 to 10 feet tall. Leaves are rough in whorls of 3 or 4 or occasionally in pairs or single. One variety has smoother leaves.

Open woods, fields.

×⅓

Lotus Lily

Nelumbo lutea　　　　　Water Lily Family　*Nymphaeaceae*

July–September　　　　Infrequent

Leaves and flowers are raised above water surface. Leaves are circular and may be more than 2 feet in diameter with the leaf stalk attached in the middle. The yellow water lilies in the genus *Nuphar* have heart-shaped leaves with stalk attached at the margin.

Quiet water.

×¾

Common Evening Primrose

Oenothera biennis   Evening Primrose Family   *Onagraceae*

July–October   Common

From 3 to 6 feet tall. Leaves are widest near base and pointed or blunt with small teeth or wavy margins, highly variable. Several of the species in this group are quite similar and difficult to separate. Work with these plants led to the mutation theory of evolution.

Roadsides, fields.

Puccoon

Lithospermum canescens   Borage Family   *Boraginaceae*

April–May   Rare

From 4 to 16 inches tall, usually with a cluster of stems per plant. Leaves are oblong, narrow, and hairy, and the lower ones are smaller. Flower color may vary from yellow to bright orange.

Open woods, rocky slopes.

×1

Flame Azalea

Rhododendron calendulaceum Heath Family *Ericaceae*

May–June Infrequent

From 4 to 10 feet tall. Leaves are oval, rounded, or pointed with a tiny spine at the tip. Flowers are in clusters and vary in color from yellow to bright orange to orange-red. This is one of our most colorful plants.

Open mountain woods.

×¾

Trumpet Vine

Campsis radicans   Bignonia Family   *Bignoniaceae*

June–July   Infrequent

A climbing vine, with leaves in pairs and divided into many pointed, toothed segments. Flower color varies from red to orange. Skin irritation has resulted from handling the plant in some persons.

Woods, thickets, roadsides.

103

×⅔

Day Lily

Hemerocallis fulva

June–July

Lily Family *Liliaceae*

Common

From 2 to 6 feet tall. Leaves are basal, long, and narrow. Flowers vary in color from yellow-orange to red-orange. Another very similar species, *H. flava*, has yellow flowers.

Roadsides, wood borders, fields.

×½

Canada Lily

Lilium canadense

June–July

Lily Family *Liliaceae*

Infrequent

From 2 to 6½ feet tall, with leaves mostly in whorls of 4 to 12 and flowers 1 to many and nodding so that open end of flower points groundward. Flower color ranges from orange to red with a varying amount of purple spotting within.

Moist wooded slopes, low thickets.

×½

Butterfly Weed

Asclepias tuberosa   Milkweed Family   *Asclepiadaceae*

June–August   Common

From 1 to 2½ feet tall. Stem usually grows at an angle. Numerous narrow, hairy leaves alternate on the stem, unlike the other milkweeds which have paired or whorled leaves. Sap is not milky like others. Flowers vary from yellow to red but are usually bright orange, making it one of the most colorful roadside plants. Poisonous if eaten.

Roadsides, fields.

× 1

Blackberry Lily

Belamcanda chinesis　　　　　　　Iris Family　*Iridaceae*

July–August　　　　　　　　　　Infrequent

From 1 to 3 feet tall. Leaves are swordlike and overlap at base like iris. This Asiatic introduction is an escape from cultivation. When the fruits ripen and open the cluster of black seeds resembles a blackberry.

Roadsides, fields.

×⅓

Turk's-cap Lily

Lilium superbum

July–August

Lily Family   *Liliaceae*

Infrequent

From 1 to 10 feet tall, with leaves in a series of whorls with some alternate on the upper stem. Flowers usually numerous and the color varying from pale orange to deep orange-red. The tiger lily, *L. tigrinum*, is similar but is easily distinguished by its alternate leaves and the presence of black bulblets in the leaf axils.

Moist woods, meadows.

×1

Spring Beauty

Claytonia caroliniana   Purslane Family   *Portulacaceae*

March–May   Common

From 1 inch to 1 foot tall, with leaves in pairs ovate to oblong and several flowers per plant. One of the showy early spring plants named for John Clayton, an early American botanist who supplied the materials for an eighteenth-century flora of Virginia. Another species, *C. virginica*, has much narrower leaves.

Rich, open wooded slopes and flood plains.

× 1¾

Storksbill

Erodium cicutarium   Geranium Family   *Geraniaceae*

March–June   Infrequent

Flowers and leaves are at ground level at first, later attaining a height of about 1 foot. Leaves are featherlike and divided into many toothed or lobed segments. Flower color varies from pale to deep pink or pinkish blue to purple.

Fields, lawns with gravel, sandy roadsides.

×¾

Robin's Plantain

Erigeron pulchellus Composite Family *Compositae*

April–May Common

From 1 to 2 feet tall. Stem and leaves are usually hairy. Most leaves are basal and wider near the tip and toothed; stem leaves are much smaller. Flower color varies from dark or light blue to pink or occasionally white.

Open wooded slopes and roadsides.

×½

Wild Geranium

Geranium maculatum   Geranium Family   *Geraniaceae*

April–June   Common

From 8 inches to 1½ feet tall. Leaves are deeply cleft into 5 to 7 segments with fingerlike lobes. Several other species of geranium are basically similar except with smaller flowers and leaves.

Woods, roadside banks.

×¾

Pink Lady's Slipper

Cypripedium acaule

April–July

Orchid Family   *Orchidaceae*

Infrequent

From 6 inches to almost 2 feet tall, with only basal leaves, no leafy stem visible. This is one of our largest orchid flowers. It may occur as scattered single plants or in large colonies.

Dry or wet woods.

×¾

Four-leaved Milkweed

Asclepias quadrifolia   Milkweed Family   *Asclepiadaceae*

May–June   Common

From 8 inches to 1½ feet tall. Leaves are in pairs except the middle ones, which are in a whorl of 4. Flower varies in color from white to pink. The several species of milkweeds all have the same general flower structure.

Open dry woods.

×1

Bleeding Heart

Dicentra eximia Poppy Family *Papaveraceae*

May–June Rare

From 8 inches to 1½ feet tall. Leaves are large and divided into many small segments. The squirrel corn, *D. canadensis*, is similar but has white or pale pink flowers. Both plants are poisonous if eaten.

Wooded or open rocky slopes or cliffs.

×1¼

Wild Pink

Silene caroliniana   Pink Family   *Caryophyllaceae*

May–June   Infrequent

From 2 to 8 inches tall. Leaves are in pairs and broadly or narrowly oblong, usually widest near the tip. The plant often grows in dense colonies. Flower color varies from white to deep red-pink.

Open rocky banks, open wood borders.

×¾

Rose Mandarin

Streptopus roseus   Lily Family   *Liliaceae*

May–June   Infrequent

From 1 to 2 feet tall. Stem is usually branched, and there are long rows of pointed leaves with the light to deep pink flowers underneath. It is sometimes called twisted stalk because occasionally the flower stalks are bent.

Rich woods.

×1¼

Showy Orchis

Orchis spectabilis   Orchid Family   *Orchidaceae*

May–June   Infrequent

From 3 to 10 inches tall. A pair of basal leaves are large and oval, sheathing the stem base. Flowers vary from white to pink-purple.

Rich woods.

×⅔

Mountain Laurel

Kalmia latifolia　　　　　　　　Heath Family　*Ericaceae*

May–July　　　　　　　　　　Common

A shrub usually 6 to 10 feet tall, with leaves thick, ever-
green, and pointed at both ends. Flowers vary from deep
pink to white. Extremely dense thickets may be formed.
They are poisonous if eaten.

Rocky wooded areas.

×½

Dame's Rocket

Hesperis matronalis Mustard Family *Cruciferae*

May–August Common

From 1 to 4 feet tall. Leaves are toothed and tapering gradually to a point; leaf stalks are short or absent. Flower color
varies from white to pink and purple. They usually occur in
colonies at times very large.

Roadsides, fields, open woods.

×³⁄₄

Spiraea

Spiraea corymbosa Rose Family *Rosaceae*

June–July Infrequent

From 1 to 3 feet tall. Leaves are oval and toothed. Flower color may be pink or white. *S. tomentosa* is somewhat similar but with flowers arranged in a spire and with the underside of the leaves densely hairy.

Roadsides, rocky slopes, stream banks.

×½

Queen of the Prairie

Filipendula rubra   Rose Family   *Rosaceae*

June—July   Rare

From 3 to 6 feet tall. Leaves are divided into several toothed and lobed segments with the terminal segment much larger. Flower color varies from pale to deep pink. Colonies of these plants grow just outside the northwest boundary of Rockbridge County.

Low roadside ditch.

×1¾

Rose Pogonia

Pogonia ophioglossoides   Orchid Family   *Orchidaceae*

June–August   Rare

From 3 inches to 2 feet tall, with 1 ovate to elliptic leaf midway up the stem and another similar but smaller leaf just under the flower. The bog rose, *Arethusa bulbosa*, is somewhat similar but develops its leaves after flowers are gone.

Open bogs.

×2

Grass Pink

Calopogon pulchellus

June–August

Orchid Family   *Orchidaceae*

Infrequent

From 10 inches to 3 feet tall, with usually 1 long narrow leaf from base of stem. Flower color varies from pink to red-purple with an occasional white.

Bogs, meadows.

×1⅓

Deptford Pink

Dianthus armeria

June–August

Pink Family   *Caryophyllaceae*

Common

From 8 inches to 2 feet tall. The entire plant is slender and somewhat rigid. Flowers are light to dark pink with very small white spots. Sweet Williams and carnations are members of this *Dianthus* group.

Roadsides, fields.

125

×1¼

White Evening Primrose

Oenothera speciosa   Evening Primrose Family   *Onagraceae*

June–August   Infrequent

From 1 to 2 feet tall. Leaves are narrow to oval, with uneven margins and often fingerlike projections near the base. Flowers vary from white to deep pink. The other members of the group have yellow flowers.

Roadsides, fields.

×¾

Purple-flowering Raspberry

Rubus odoratus   Rose Family   *Rosaceae*

June–August   Common

From 3 to 6 feet tall. Leaves are broad with 3 to 5 triangular lobes having toothed margins. Flower color varies from pale pink to deep pink-purple. This is the only member of the blackberry-raspberry group that we have with no prickles and with leaves that are not divided into several segments.

Wood borders, roadsides, streambanks.

×1

Crown Vetch

Coronilla varia

Bean Family *Leguminosae*

June–September

Common

From 1 to 2 feet tall. Stems are erect or trailing, leaves are divided into small segments, and flowers vary from pale pink to deep pink with some purple. This is a European escape from cultivation. The seeds have been reported as poisonous.

Roadsides, fields.

×¾

Star Thistle

Centaurea maculosa

June–October

Composite Family *Compositae*

Common

From 1 to 4 feet tall. Leaves are divided into very slender segments. Flower heads vary in color from pale to deep pink to pink-purple. The several other species in this group have narrow leaves and similar flower heads.

Roadsides, fields, pastures.

Nodding Wild Onion

Allium cernuum   Lily Family   *Liliaceae*

July–August   Common

From 8 inches to 2 feet tall. Leaves are basal, narrow, and grasslike; flowering stem curves downward just beneath flowers. Flower color varies from purple to pink to white.

Open woods, rocky slopes and ledges.

×⅔

Wild Bergamot

Monarda fistulosa　　　　　　　Mint Family　*Labiatae*

July–August　　　　　　　　　　Common

From 1 to 4 feet tall, with leaves in pairs, triangular and toothed. Leaves immediately under flower head are often pinkish. *M. clinopodia* is similar but without the tufts of hairs on the tips of the upper part of the flowers.

Woods, wood borders, roadside banks.

×1

Swamp Milkweed

Asclepias incarnata   Milkweed Family   *Asclepiadaceae*

July–August   Common

From 2 to 4 feet tall, usually branched, with numerous gradually tapering leaves widest near the base and in pairs. Flower color varies from pale pink to deep pink-red. The kinds of milkweed are rather easily identified as members of the group by their common and distinctive floral structure.

Streamsides, swamps.

× 1¼

Rose Pink

Sabatia angularis   Gentian Family   *Gentianaceae*

July–August   Common

From 8 inches to 2½ feet tall. Stem is winged; ovate leaves
in pairs are pointed or blunt. Flowers are deep pink with a
green star in center occasionally varying to white.

Moist woods, marshes, fields.

×⅓

Joe-pye Weed

Eupatorium fistulosum   Composite Family   *Compositae*

July–September   Common

From 4 to 7 feet tall, with hollow stems and leaves in whorls
of 4 to 7. Flower color varies from pink to purple. *E. dubium*
is similar but with densely resinous-dotted leaves beneath.
E. purpureum and *E. maculatum* are also similar but with solid
stems, and the latter has flat-topped flowering arrangement.

Moist woods, marshes.

×1

Soapwort

Saponaria officinalis   Pink Family   *Caryophyllaceae*

July–October   Common

From 1 to 3 feet tall. Leaves are in pairs elliptic or ovate with blunt or pointed tips. Flower color varies from white to deep pink. The material in the sap that causes lather when mixed with water is also poisonous.

Roadsides, fields.

×⅓

Toadshade

Trillium sessile   Lily Family   *Liliaceae*

April–May   Rare

From 4 inches to 1 foot tall. Leaves may be all green or mottled. The maroon petals are erect rather than spreading. *T. erectum* is similar having the same color but stalked flowers.

Moist woods.

136

×2

Bird-on-the-wing

Polygala paucifolia   Milkwort Family   *Polygalaceae*

May–June   Rare

From 2 to 6 inches tall, with a few oval-shaped leaves just beneath the flowers and scalelike lower stem leaves. Flowers are pink-purple to purplish red or occasionally white. The plant usually occurs in small to extensive colonies.

Moist woods or wood borders.

×1⅓

Wild Coffee

Triosteum aurantiacum   Honeysuckle Family   *Caprifoliaceae*

May–June   Infrequent

From 1 to 4 feet tall. Leaves are in pairs with 1 or 2 middle pairs narrowly connected across the stem. Flowers are usually bright to dull orange-red. There is disagreement regarding number of species. *T. perfoliatum* has broadly connected leaves and red-brown flowers; *T. angustifolium* has narrower leaves and yellow flowers.

Open woods or clearings.

×¾

Indian Paint Brush

Castilleja coccinea   Figwort Family   *Scrophulariaceae*

May–July   Infrequent

From 1 to 2 feet tall. Reduced leaves beneath the flowers are scarlet along with the lower part of the flowers; lower leaves are green and usually divided into 3 segments. The plant is a partial parasite usually upon the roots of grasses.

Roadsides, fields, open wood borders.

139

×1

Trumpet Honeysuckle

Lonicera sempervirens   Honeysuckle Family   *Caprifoliaceae*

May–July   Infrequent

A climbing vine with paired, oval leaves white or whitish beneath. The first 1 or 2 pairs of leaves are fused around the stem. Wild honeysuckle, *L. dioica*, is similar, but the flowers are greenish yellow or dull red and cleft into two lips.

Woods, thickets.

×1

Poppy

Papaver dubium   Poppy Family   *Papaveraceae*

May–July   Infrequent

From 1 to 2 feet tall. Stem is slender usually without branching; leaves are narrow and much divided into slender toothed segments. Another species, *P. somniferum*, is the source of poppy seeds in bread-making and also the source of opium.

Roadsides, fields.

×¾

Fire Pink

Silene virginica

May–July

Pink Family   *Caryophyllaceae*

Common

From 8 inches to 2 feet tall. Leaves are in pairs, often wider near the tip. They often grow in fairly extensive colonies, providing some of the most vivid color of our flora.

Open woods and wood borders.

142

×½

Golden Seal

Hydrastis canadensis　　　　Crowfoot Family　*Ranunculaceae*

June–July (fruiting)　　　　Rare

From 8 inches to 2 feet tall, with usually 1 basal and 2 stem leaves broadly heart-shaped and 5-lobed. The greenish white flower is present in April or May and has a tassellike appearance. The plant is poisonous if eaten. It has been very nearly eliminated by the extensive collection for medicinal use.

Woods.

×2

Scarlet Pimpernel

Anagallis arvensis Primrose Family *Primulaceae*

June–August Infrequent

From 4 inches to 1 foot tall, with stems usually trailing along the ground and ovate leaves in pairs without stalks. Flower color varies from orange-red to scarlet with an occasional blue or white. It is reputed to have varied powers: a medical cure-all, mental stimulant, weather prophet. Handling of the plant sometimes results in skin irritation.

Roadsides, fields, lawns.

× 1¼

Sheep Sorrel

Rumex acetosella   Buckwheat Family   *Polygonaceae*

June–August   Common

From 8 inches to 1½ feet tall. Leaves are variable but generally resemble a spear point, arrowhead, or sword blade.
Flowers vary from greenish yellow to red or purple. These
plants often grow in extensive colonies. The leaves are sometimes used as salad greens. These plants are indicative of acid
soil.

Roadsides, fields, pastures.

Cardinal Flower

Lobelia cardinalis Bluebell Family *Campanulaceae*

July–September Infrequent

From 1 to 6 feet tall, with numerous leaves tapered at both ends and toothed. *L. siphilitica* is similar with blue and smaller flowers. White flowers may occasionally be found.

Streamsides, marshes, low woods.

×1

Ground Ivy

Glechoma hederacea   Mint Family   *Labiatae*

March–June   Common

From 4 to 8 inches tall. Leaves, in pairs, are kidney-shaped
to almost round and toothed or scalloped. The creeping
stems usually form dense mats often as extensive ground
cover. It has been used both as a flavoring and a medicine.

Woods, roadsides, fields.

×¾

Common Blue Violet

Viola papilionacea   Violet Family   *Violaceae*

March–June   Common

From 2 to 8 inches tall. Flowers are usually a little over-topped by the heart-shaped leaves, which may be 3 to 5 inches wide. Flowers are commonly deep blue to violet with a light center. The color form shown here is called Confederate violet.

Moist woods, fields, roadsides, lawns.

Dwarf Larkspur

Delphinium tricorne   Crowfoot Family   *Ranunculaceae*

April–May   Infrequent

From 1 to 2 feet tall. Leaves are deeply cleft and divided into narrow segments. Flower color varies from deep purple to pale blue and white. *D. exaltatum* is taller with leaves divided into fewer and wider segments. *D. ajacis* has leaves divided into extremely narrow segments. All the larkspurs are poisonous if eaten.

Rich wooded slopes, especially limestone areas.

×1

Crested Dwarf Iris

Iris cristata

April–May

Iris Family   *Iridaceae*

Common

From 1 to 3 inches tall. Leaves are swordlike, flower color varies from blue to violet, and stem is underground but usually partly exposed. *I. verna* is very similar but does not have the crest (ridged white-yellow streaks) on the outer flower parts. Iris plants in general cause skin irritation in some individuals.

Rich woods, slopes, and stream banks.

Bluebells

Mertensia virginica

April–May

Borage Family *Boraginaceae*

Rare

From 1 to 2 feet tall. Leaves are 3 to 10 inches long, buds are pink, and flowers vary from light to dark blue or occasionally white. There is usually a cluster of stems per plant. Small to large colonies are often found.

Stream banks, low moist woods.

151

×1

Grape Hyacinth

Muscari racemosum   Lily Family   *Liliaceae*

April–May   Infrequent

From 2 to 10 inches tall. Flowers are blue or violet, sometimes white. Leaves are almost cylindrical. Another species, *M. botryoides*, is very similar but has flat leaves.

Fields, lawns, roadsides.

×½

Blue Phlox

Phlox divaricata   Phlox Family   *Polemoniaceae*

April–May   Infrequent

From 8 inches to about 1½ feet tall. Flower color varies from
pale blue to purple with an occasional white or pinkish blue.
Other phlox species are generally similar except flower color
is usually pink to red-purple, and some are low-growing.

Rich woods, rocky wooded slopes, wood borders.

× 1⅓

Periwinkle

Vinca minor Dogbane Family *Apocynaceae*

April–May Infrequent

A low vine, with leaves opposite on the stem and a shiny, deep green. Flowers are light blue to blue-violet. It usually forms a fairly dense ground cover. Another species, *V. major*, has slightly larger flowers and leaves with a hairy margin. Both are European escapes from cultivation.

Roadsides, fields, wood borders.

×¾

Jacob's Ladder

Polemonium reptans

April–May

Phlox Family *Polemoniaceae*

Rare

From 8 inches to 1½ feet tall. Leaves are long and divided into several to many pairs of small segments. Flowers are usually deep blue but may be white.

Rich woods.

155

×1

Bluets

Houstonia caerulea

April–June

Madder Family   *Rubiaceae*

Common

From 2 to 6 inches tall. Leaves are in pairs with upper leaves stalkless and the lower stalked. Flowers vary from blue to almost white. *H. patens* is similar with flowers darker with a dark center. *H. serpyllifolia* has prostrate stems. *H. purpurea*, *H. longifolia*, and *H. tenuifolia* have several flowers on each stalk, and the last two have very narrow leaves.

Open woods, streamsides, fields.

×1¾

Bird-foot Violet

Viola pedata Violet Family *Violaceae*

April–June Common

From 2 to 6 inches tall. Leaves are divided into 7 to 13 fingerlike segments. Flowers may vary from light blue to blue-purple, or the two upper petals may be dark purple with the lower ones being the usual blue or purple. This is one of the most showy violets.

Roadsides, open woods, fields.

×¾

Venus's Looking-glass

Specularia perfoliata   Bluebell Family   *Campanulaceae*

May–June   Common

From 1 to 3 feet tall, with very straight, usually unbranched, leaves clasping the stem. *S. biflora* is similar except that the leaves do not clasp the stem, and more often few if any flowers are open.

Open woods, fields, roadsides.

×½

Wild Comfrey

Cynoglossum virginianum   Borage Family   *Boraginaceae*

May–June   Infrequent

From 1 to 3 feet tall, with several large basal leaves and smaller leaves about halfway up the stem. All leaves are rough with bristly hairs. Flowers vary from blue to white. Hound's tongue, *C. officinale*, is similar except for red flowers and leaves all the way up the stem.

Open woods, wood borders.

×¾

Wild Lupine

Lupinus perrenis   Bean Family   *Leguminosae*

May–June   Infrequent

From 8 inches to 2 feet tall. Leaves are divided into 7 to 11 fingerlike segments. Flowers are usually blue but may vary to pinkish or occasionally white. This species is poisonous, especially the seeds.

Open woods, wood borders, roadsides.

×1½

One-flowered Cancer-root

Orobanche uniflora   Broom-rape Family   *Orobanchaceae*

May–June   Infrequent

From 2 to 3 inches tall. Leaves are scalelike at base of stem,
one flower per stem. Flowers vary from white to blue-violet.
These plants are parasitic upon the roots of other plants.

Rich woods.

×1½

Miami Mist

Phacelia purshii   Waterleaf Family   *Hydrophyllaceae*

May–June   Rare

From 4 inches to 1½ feet tall. Leaves are hairy and have pointed lobes. Flowers are fringed and blue with a yellowish green center. *P. fimbriata* is very similar but with white flowers. *P. dubia* has smaller flowers without the fringe.

Streamsides, moist woods, low roadsides.

× 1¼

Nettle-leaved Sage

Salvia urticifolia   Mint Family   *Labiatae*

May–July   Common

From 1 to 1½ feet tall. Leaves are in pairs and broadly rounded-triangular and toothed. Cancer weed, *S. lyrata*, is somewhat similar with the exception that the leaves are basal only.

Open woods, clearings.

163

× 1¾

Blue-eyed Grass

Sisyrinchium angustifolium Iris Family *Iridaceae*

May–July Common

From 4 inches to 1½ feet tall. Leaves appear grasslike, but a closer look shows the resemblance to miniature iris leaves. Flower color varies from light blue to violet. The several species are easily recognized as members of the group.

Open woods, clearings, low roadsides.

×1

Forget-me-not

Myosotis scorpioides   Borage Family   *Boraginaceae*

May–August   Infrequent

Stems are 1 to 2 feet long, usually partially erect and partially lying on the ground. Leaves are oblong and narrow. This is a European introduction often cultivated. *M. laxa* is similar but with paler blue and smaller flowers.

Streamsides or shallow water.

×1¼

Spiderwort

Tradescantia virginiana   Spiderwort Family   *Commelinaceae*

May–August   Infrequent

From 8 inches to 2 feet tall. Leaves are long and narrow, appearing grasslike. Flowers vary from blue to purple. *T. ohioensis* is very similar except for the flower stalks being smooth rather than hairy.

Roadsides, wood borders.

× 1¾

Common Speedwell

Veronica officinalis   Figwort Family   *Scrophulariaceae*

May–August   Common

From 4 inches to 1 foot tall. Stems are prostrate with the flowering branches erect. Flowers vary from light to dark blue. *V. anagallis-aquatica* and *V. americana* are less common and found in wet places; the former has stalkless upper leaves while those of the latter are stalked.

Open woods, fields, roadsides.

× 1¾

Heal-all

Prunella vulgaris   Mint Family *Labiatae*

May–October   Common

From 4 inches to 2 feet tall, often branched. Leaves are in pairs, oval with rounded or pointed tips, and variable in size and shape with identification being aided by stable flower structure and arrangement. As the name indicates, it was once thought to be a cure for many ailments.

Roadsides, fields, lawns.

×⅔

Horse Nettle

Solanum carolinense   Nightshade Family   *Solanaceae*

May–October   Common

From 6 inches to 3 feet tall. Stem and leaves are spiny; leaves are irregularly toothed or lobed. Flower color varies from white to pale blue or purple. This species, like most members of the group, is poisonous if eaten. The green parts of the Irish potato, *S. tuberosum*, are poisonous if eaten.

Roadsides, fields, pastures.

× 1¼

Skullcap

Scutellaria integrifolia   Mint Family   *Labiatae*

June–July   Common

From 8 inches to 2½ feet tall. Basal leaves are stalked and ovate or triangular with rounded teeth; upper leaves are shorter-stalked and more elongated with smooth margins. All members of this group have a ridge on the upper side of flower base.

Open woods, wood borders, roadsides.

×¾

Bellflower

Campanula rapunculoides   Bluebell Family   *Campanulaceae*

June–August   Infrequent

From 2 to 5 feet tall. Leaves are long-stalked and ovate becoming narrower at stem base, short-stalked and gradually
tapering to a point on the upper stem. This is a European
introduction escaped from gardens. *C. divaricata* is a native
bellflower that is much taller and more branched with very
small blue flowers in a branching arrangement.

Roadsides, fields.

171

×1

Viper's Bugloss

Echium vulgare   Borage Family   *Boraginaceae*

June–August   Common

From 1 to 3 feet tall. Basal leaves are long and narrow, stem leaves are smaller, and the entire plant is bristly. Flowers vary from dark to light blue. This plant may cause skin irritation when handled.

Roadsides, fields.

Pale-spike Lobelia

Lobelia spicata   Bluebell Family   *Campanulaceae*

June–August   Common

From 8 inches to 3 feet tall. Leaves are oblong, often with the widest part nearer the tip, their margins are wavy or toothed, and upper leaves are much reduced. Flower color varies from pale blue to white.

Woods, fields.

Monkey Flower

Mimulus ringens   Figwort Family   *Scrophulariaceae*

June–September   Common

From 2 to 4 feet tall. Leaves are in pairs without stalks, vary from elliptic to ovate, and are either pointed or blunt. *M. alatus* is very similar but has stalked leaves.

Streamsides, marshes, bogs.

×2¼

Dayflower

Commelina communis   Spiderwort Family   *Commelinaceae*

June–October   Common

From 6 inches to 2 feet tall. Leaves are ovate and somewhat thick with the base sheathing the stem. *C. diffusa* is similar but all 3 petals are blue. *C. erecta* and *C. virginica* have the leaves sheathing the flower fused at the base, and the latter also has all blue petals.

Moist woods, roadsides.

175

×½

Chicory

Cichorium intybus   Composite Family   *Compositae*

June–October   Common

From 1 to 6 feet tall. Basal leaves are somewhat similar to dandelion, upper stem leaves are much smaller, and flowers are usually blue but may be white. Roots are used to add flavor to coffee, but it gives an unwanted flavor to cow's milk.

Roadsides, fields.

×¾

Tall Bellflower

Campanula americana   Bluebell Family   *Campanulaceae*

July–September   Common

From 1½ to 6 feet tall. Stem is usually unbranched. Leaves taper at both ends and are toothed. Flower color varies from light blue to dark blue or violet. This species differs from the other bellflowers in not forming a bell.

Rich woods, wood borders, roadside banks.

×¾

Teasel

Dipsacus sylvestris Teasel Family *Dipsacaceae*

July–September Common

From 3 to 10 feet tall. Stems and leaves are prickly; leaves are in pairs, large, and sometimes fused around the stem. Flowers may be blue-pink or white. Flowers develop in the middle of the flowering head and spread upward and downward. Heads are often used in dried arrangements.

Roadsides, fields, meadows.

×½

Heartleaf

Asarum virginicum   Birthwort Family   *Aristolochiaceae*

March–May   Common

Leaves are usually more or less on the ground covering a cluster of flowers. Leaves have a spicy odor when bruised. This species differs from wild ginger, *A. canadense*, in the smooth leaves and leaf stalks. Another smooth heartleaf, *A. arifolia*, has more triangular leaves.

Woods and rocky slopes.

×¾

Purple Dead-nettle

Lamium purpureum   Mint Family   *Labiatae*

March–May   Common

From 4 to 12 inches tall. Leaves are heart-shaped and in pairs; upper leaves are crowded on the stem and frequently purple and lower leaves have longer stalks. Flower color varies from bluish red to purple. *L. amplexicaule* has stalkless leaves and spotted flowers.

Roadsides, fields.

× 2/3

Wild Ginger

Asarum canadense   Birthwort Family   *Aristolochiaceae*

April–May   Infrequent

From 6 to 10 inches tall. Flower is at ground level or under leaf litter usually between two leaves. Bruised parts have the odor of ginger. Leaf contact causes skin irritation in some individuals.

Rich woods.

×1

Dutchman's Pipe

Aristolochia durior Birthwort Family *Aristolochiaceae*

May–June Infrequent

Climbing vine. Leaves are heart-shaped and large (6 to 10 inches long and wide). The twining vine may climb to the tops of tall trees and resemble large grapevines. Flowers (the "pipes") may vary from green to purple.

Rich woods.

×1

Waterleaf

Hydrophyllum virginianum   Waterleaf Family   *Hydrophyllaceae*

May–June   Infrequent

From 8 inches to 2 feet tall. Leaves are divided into 5 to 7 toothed segments. Flowers vary from white to dark purple.

Rich woods, moist wooded slopes and wood borders.

×¾

Beard Tongue

Penstemon canescens   Figwort Family   *Scrophulariaceae*

May–June   Common

From 1 to 3 feet tall. Leaves are narrowly triangular in shape and in pairs with their bases clasping the stem. Flowers have an inflated appearance and vary from deep purple to almost white.

Open woods, roadside banks, fields.

184

×¾

Swordleaf Phlox

Phlox buckleyi Phlox Family *Polemoniaceae*

May–June Rare

From 6 inches to 1½ feet tall. Leaves are in pairs and very narrow and sharp-pointed with hairs. Upper stem, flower stalks, and flowers are densely covered with hairs enlarged at their tips. This species is apparently endemic to western Virginia and eastern West Virginia.

Open gravelly banks.

×1½

Violet Wood Sorrel

Oxalis violacea　　　　　Wood Sorrel Family　*Oxalidaceae*

May–July　　　　　　　Infrequent

From 4 to 8 inches tall, with stem underground, flower stalk and leaves arising from soil surface, and leaves divided into three notched segments. Flower color varies from pinkish purple to violet or white. The small leaflike lobes at base of flower have enlarged orange tips. *O. montana* is similar without the orange tips on the parts forming the base of the flower.

Rich woods, stream borders.

×¾

Rosebay

Rhododendron catawbiense

June

Heath Family *Ericaceae*

Common

From 3 to 10 feet tall. Leaves are rounded at both ends. The large, clustered, pink to blue-purple flowers make one of the most colorful displays of the region. *R. maximum* has less showy white flowers. Both are internally poisonous.

Mountain woods.

187

× 1½

Climbing Milkweed

Gonolobus obliquus   Milkweed Family   *Asclepiadaceae*

June–July   Infrequent

A climbing vine with oval to round leaves. Flowers are purple inside and greenish outside. The fruits are spiny; often last year's fruits will be present. The other climbing milkweeds are generally similar. *G. gonocarpos* usually has much less rounded leaves, yellowish flowers, and smooth fruits.

Woody rocky slopes, thick wood borders.

×¾

Leather Flower

Clematis viorna   Crowfoot Family   *Ranunculaceae*

June–August   Infrequent

A climbing vine. Leaves, in pairs, are divided into 3 to 7 segments. *C. ochroleuca* is a small rare plant with a similar but yellow flower. *C. virginiana* is a common vine with clusters of white flowers and feathery-appearing fruits; leaf segments are toothed.

Dry or moist woods and wood borders, rocky slopes.

×1¼

Vervain

Verbena simplex

June–August

Vervain Family   *Verbenanceae*

Infrequent

From 8 inches to 2 feet tall. Leaves are narrow and toothed, pointed at both ends. Flowers vary from pink to purple.

Roadsides, open rocky slopes.

190

× 1¼

Nightshade

Solanum dulcamara

June–September

Nightshade Family *Solanaceae*

Rare

A climbing vine to 10 or 12 feet or trailing along the ground. Leaves are ovate, usually with lobes at the base. The fruits are bright red berries. The plant has a disagreeable odor and is poisonous if eaten. The Irish potato and eggplant are members of this group.

Moist roadsides, wood borders, streamsides.

×¾

Bull Thistle

Cirsium vulgare Composite Family *Compositae*

June–September Common

From 2 to 6 feet tall. The plant is spiny throughout. Leaves are divided into many segments all toothed and spiny. Frequently growing in dense, impassable colonies, it is a European introduction that presents a serious weed problem. *Carduus nutans* is similar but with nodding flower heads.

Pastures, fields, roadsides.

×¾

Passion Flower

Passiflora incarnata　　　Passion Flower Family　*Passifloraceae*

June–September　　　Common

A trailing or climbing vine. Leaves are divided into 3 large pointed lobes with small teeth. The yellowish fruits, called maypops, are edible. The various parts of the unusual floral structure have been described as symbolic of the Crucifixion. *P. lutea* is similar but with rounded leaf lobes and yellow and smaller flowers.

Roadsides, fields.

×1

Bachelor's Button

Centaurea cyanus Composite Family *Compositae*

June–September Infrequent

From 1 to 3 feet tall. Leaves are long and narrow; some of the lower ones may be lobed. The entire plant is whitish or light green. Flower color is usually blue or purple but may be pink or white.

Roadsides, fields.

194

×⅔

Common Morning Glory

Ipomoea purpurea　　　Morning Glory Family　*Convolvulaceae*

July–September　　　Common

A twining vine. Leaves are broadly heart-shaped to almost round. Flowers may be white, blue, purple, red, or a mixture of these colors. *I. lacunosa* has smaller flowers. *I. hederacea* has deeply lobed leaves. *I. pandurata* has white flowers with a red or purple center and frequently lobed leaves. The sweet potato is a member of this group.

Fields, roadsides.

×½

Ironweed

Vernonia noveboracensis   Composite Family   *Compositae*

July–September   Common

From 2 to 7 feet tall. Leaves are slightly or much wider near the base and gradually taper to a point with the margins smooth or toothed.

Moist woods, marshes, streamsides.

×1

Monkshood

Aconitum uncinatum   Crowfoot Family   *Ranunculaceae*

August–September   Rare

From 2 to 4 feet tall, often leaning on other plants. Leaves are divided into 3 or 5 lobes with irregular teeth. *A. reclinatum* is similar but with white or yellowish white flowers.

Rich woods.

Pink Fumewort

Corydalis sempervirens   Poppy Family   *Papaveraceae*

April–May   Infrequent

From 6 inches to almost 3 feet tall. Leaves are long-stalked at base and without stalks higher up the stem, the blades many-lobed. There is another species, *C. flavula*, with smaller all-yellow flowers. Sheep and cattle are poisoned by this plant.

Steep, rocky slopes and open rocky areas.

×¾

Wild Columbine

Aquilegia canadensis   Crowfoot Family   *Ranunculaceae*

April–August   Common

From 1 to 3 feet tall. Leaves in division of 3 segments. Flowers may vary in the amount of flare and in color but are easily recognized. Another species, *A. vulgaris*, is an escape from cultivation, having blue and white flowers.

Steep, rocky slopes, open woods, roadsides.

× 1½

Goat's Rue

Tephrosia virginiana   Bean Family   *Leguminosae*

June–July   Common

From 1 to 2 feet tall, generally covered with white or grayish
white hairs. Leaves are divided into many narrow and pointed
segments. Flower color may vary from yellow and pink to
yellow and purple.

Roadsides, fields, open woods.

Pronunciation Key to Scientific Names

The symbols ` and ´ mark the syllable to be accented; the former calls for a long vowel sound, while the latter calls for a short vowel sound.

Acanthàceae
Justícia americàna
Amaryllidàceae
Hypóxis hirsùta
Anacardiàceae
Rhùs radìcans
Apocynàceae
Vínca mìnor
Aràceae
Arisaèma triphýllum
Araliàceae
Pànax quinquefòlius
Aristolochiàceae
Aristolòchia dùrior
Ásarum canadénse
Ásarum virgínicum
Asclepiadàceae
Asclèpias incarnàta
Asclèpias quadrifòlia
Asclèpias tuberòsa
Gonólobus oblìquus
Balsaminàceae
Impàtiens pállida
Berberidàceae
Caulophýllum thalictroìdes
Jeffersònia diphýlla
Podophýllum peltàtum
Bignoniàceae
Cámpsis radìcans
Boraginàceae
Cynoglóssum virginiànum
Échium vulgàre
Lithospérmum canéscens
Merténsia virgínica
Myosòtis scorpioìdes
Cactàceae
Opúntia humifùsa
Campanulàceaè
Campánula americàna

Campánula rapunculoìdes
Lobèlia cardinális
Lobèlia spicàta
Speculària perfoliàta
Caprifoliàceae
Lonícera sempérvirens
Triósteum aurantìacum
Caryophyllàceae
Diánthus armèria
Saponària officinàlis
Silène caroliniàna
Silène stellàta
Silène virgínica
Stellària pùbera
Commelinàceae
Commelìna commùnis
Tradescántia virginiàna
Compósitae
Achillèa millefòlium
Antennària plantaginifòlia
Centaurèa cỳanus
Centaurèa maculòsa
Chrysánthemum leucánthemum
Crysógonum virginiànum
Cichòrium íntybus
Círsium vulgàre
Coreópsis verticillàta
Erígeron pulchéllus
Eupatòrium fistulòsum
Hieràcium venòsum
Parthénium integrifòlium
Rudbéckia hírta
Senécio aùreus
Sílphium trifoliàtum
Taráxacum officinàle
Tragopògon màjor
Tussilàgo fárfara
Vernònia noveboracénsis
Convolvulàceae

Convólvulus sèpium
Convólvulus spithamàeus
Ipomoèa purpúrea
Crassulàceae
  Sèdum ternàtum
Crucíferae
  Alliària officinàlis
  Dentària laciniàta
  Hésperis matronàlis
  Nastúrtium officinàle
Dipsacàceae
  Dípsacus sylvéstris
Diapensiàceae
  Gàlax aphýlla
Ericàceae
  Gaulthèria procúmbens
  Kálmia latifòlia
  Rhododéndron calendulàceum
  Rhododéndron catawbiénse
  Vaccìnium stamíneum
Euphorbiàceae
  Euphórbia corollàta
Gentianàceae
  Sabàtia angulàris
Geraniàceae
  Eródium cicutàrium
  Geránium maculàtum
Gramíneae
  Hýstrix pátula
Guttíferae
  Hyperìcum perforàtum
Hydrophyllàceae
  Hydrophýllum virginiànum
  Phacèlia púrshii
Iridàceae
  Belamcánda chinénsis
  Ìris cristàta
  Sisyrínchium angustifòlium
Labìatae
  Glechòma hederàcea
  Làmium purpùreum
  Monárda fistulòsa
  Prunélla vulgàris
  Sálvia urticifòlia
  Scutellària integrifòlia
Leguminòsae
  Baptísia tinctòria
  Cássia hebecárpa
  Coronílla vària

Lupìnus perénnis
Melilòtus officinàlis
Tephròsia virginiàna
Vícia caroliniàna
Liliàceae
  Állium cérnuum
  Amiánthium muscaetóxicum
  Clintònia umbellulàta
  Convallària majàlis
  Erythrònium americànum
  Hemerocállis fúlva
  Lílium canadénse
  Lílium supérbum
  Maiánthemum canadénse
  Medèola virginiàna
  Muscàri racemòsum
  Ornithógalum umbellàtum
  Polygónatum biflòrum
  Smilacìna racemòsa
  Smìlax herbàcea
  Stréptopus ròseus
  Tríllium grandiflòrum
  Tríllium séssile
  Uvulària grandiflòra
  Veràtrum víride
  Yúcca filamentòsa
Malvàceae
  Málva rotundifòlia
Nymphaeàceae
  Nelúmbo lùtea
Onagràceae
  Oenothèra biénnis
  Oenothèra fruticòsa
  Oenothèra speciòsa
Orchidàceae
  Calopògon pulchéllus
  Cypripèdium acaùle
  Cypripèdium calcèolus
  Órchis spectábilis
  Pogònia ophioglossòides
  Spiránthes grácilis
  Tipulària díscolor
Orobanchàceae
  Conópholis americàna
  Orobánche uniflòra
Oxalidàceae
  Óxalis violàcea
Papaveràceae
  Chelidònium màjus

202

Corýdalis sempérvirens
Dicéntra cucullària
Dicéntra exímia
Papàver dùbium
Sanguinària canadénsis
Passifloràceae
Passiflòra incarnàta
Polemoniàceae
Phlóx búckleyi
Phlóx divaricàta
Polemònium réptans
Polygalàceae
Polýgala paucifòlia
Polygonàceae
Rùmex acetosélla
Portulacàceae
Claytònia caroliniàna
Primulàceae
Anagállis arvénsis
Lysimáchia quadrifòlia
Pyrolàceae
Chimáphila maculàta
Monótropa hypópithys
Monótropa uniflòra
Ranunculàceae
Aconìtum uncinàtum
Actaèa pachýpoda
Anemonélla thalictroìdes
Aquilègia canadénsis
Cáltha palústris
Cimicífuga racemòsa
Clématis viórna
Delphínium tricórne
Hepática acutíloba
Hydrástis canadénsis
Ranùnculus bulbòsus
Trautvettèria caroliniénsis
Rhamnàceae
Ceanòthus americànus
Rosàceae
Arúncus dioìcus
Filipéndula rùbra

Fragària virginiàna
Gillènia trifoliàta
Potentílla récta
Rùbus odoràtus
Spiraèa corymbòsa
Rubiàceae
Cephalánthus occidentàlis
Houstònia caerùlea
Santalàceae
Comándra umbellàta
Saxifragàceae
Mitélla diphýlla
Tiarélla cordifòlia
Scrophulariàceae
Castillèja coccínea
Gerárdia virgínica
Linària vulgàris
Mímulus ríngens
Pediculàris canadénsis
Penstémon canéscens
Verbáscum blattària
Verbáscum thápsus
Verónica officinàlis
Solanàceae
Datùra stramònium
Solànum carolinénse
Solànum dulcamàra
Umbellíferae
Daúcus caròta
Heraclèum máximum
Osmorhìza clàytoni
Pastinàca satìva
Zízia áptera
Urticàceae
Urtìca dioìca
Verbenàceae
Verbèna símplex
Violàceae
Vìola canadénsis
Vìola papilionàcea
Vìola pedàta
Vìola pensylvánica

Index of Common and Scientific Names